Still Dancing

Still Dancing

poems

by

Michael J. Wilson

First Edition

Hidden Brook Press
www.HiddenBrookPress.com
HiddenBrookPress@gmail.com
EST. 1994

Still Dancing
by Michael J. Wilson

Editor:John B. Lee
Cover Image: Michael's mother, Carol Wilson-Green
Cover Design: Paul Wilson wogz187@gmail.com
    Ascina Illustration & Design
    www.facebook.com/AscinaIllustrationsandDesign
Layout and Design: Richard M. Grove

Typeset in Calibri
Printed and bound in Canada
Distributed in USA by Ingram,
        in Canada by Hidden Brook Distribution

Library and Archives Canada Cataloguing in Publication

Title: Still dancing / poems by Michael J. Wilson.
Names: Wilson, Michael J., 1958- author.
Description: Series statement: The John B. Lee signature series
Identifiers: Canadiana 20220135894 | ISBN 9781989786284 (softcover)
Classification: LCC PS8595.I5842 S75 2021 | DDC C811/.54—dc23

for Della

Acknowledgements

A version of "Waiting For The Engine To Cool" first appeared in the photo-essay, *Men Of Iron Fish*, by Port Stanley Photographer, Jan Row; "The Southern Dunwich Jefferson Salamander" first appeared in *U. of Windsor Review*; "Fisherman's Beach" and "Crow Country" first appeared in the anthology, *The Beauty Of Being Elsewhere* (Hidden Brook Press), edited by John B. Lee.

Special thanks to:

Frank and Nancy Prothero, for welcoming a young fisherman/poet into the community of Port Stanley by publishing some of my earliest poems in the village newspaper. Their encouragement and support over the following years helped me steer, and keep, a steady course; **Navtej Bharati,** a wise and kind man, for publishing my first book; **Jim Rowan**, who filmed and edited a fine documentary about the fishing culture on Lake Erie, weaving my poetry throughout; the dedicated staff at London's Parkwood Hospital, especially **Scott Maclain**, for three years of twice-a-week home therapy; and my social worker, **Bob Lomax**. Without their aid, I might've given up; my wife, **Della**, for unwavering support and contributing the author-bio; my mom, **Carole,** for her painting adorning the book's cover; my photographer daughter, **Alissa,** for the author photo; my son, **Paul,** whose technical assistance, and wise advice, literally made this book happen; my friend and mentor, **John B. Lee,** for inviting me to put a manuscript together for his signature series highlighting work by some truly fine poets. I am humbly honoured to be among such company; my publisher, **Richard (Tai) Grove,** and the staff at Hidden Brook Press; my dear friends and fellow poets of **The London Group**; and the sturdy men, women, and families of the fishing community that I had the pleasure to work with for so many years.

Contents

Souvenirs

- Bookends – *p. 3*
- The Spring Street Gang – *p. 5*
- Friday Night at the Clifton Hotel – *p. 6*
- Going to Work – *p. 7*
- Just Another Day on Lake Erie – *p. 8*
- When – *p. 9*
- Waiting for the Engine to Cool – *p. 10*
- More to the Story – *p. 1* 5
- The Work of Art – *p. 1* 9
- Jackie Grayling – *p. 21*
- Robert 'Silly" Tilly – *p. 23*
- Fisherman's Beach – *p. 25*
- Tough-Guys – *p. 26*
- A Near-Death Experience – *p. 27*
- All She Really Needed – *p. 28*
- A Love Story – *p. 29*
- Lake Erie, My Lake – *p. 30*

Stagecraft

– Rathering – *p. 32*
– The Southern Dunwich Jefferson Salamander – *p. 33*
– Two Trees and a Spider – *p. 36*
– Woodlots – *p. 37*
– (A Sheaf of Sonnets:) Drama at the Beach – *p. 39*
– Mimicking – *p. 40*
– First Tomato – *p. 41*
– Crow Country – *p. 42*
– Afterglow – *p. 43*
– Lust, As Love With Need – *p. 44*
– Woodstock Festival, 1969 – *p. 45*
– New Moon – *p. 46*
– Post-Glacial – *p. 48*
– Attending An Outdoor Book-Launch – *p. 49*
– If – *p. 50*
– Sapiens Sapiens – *p. 52*
– Angels Fallenly – *p. 53*
– Original Sin – *p. 54*
– Standing Before His Maker – *p. 55*
– Poem Split in Two – *p. 56*
– Autobiography of My Legs – *p. 60*
– A Final Word – *p. 62*

Author Bio – *p. 64*

Souvenirs

Bookends

I

Leaving the city
to its academics and street violence,
the city of his parents, he wholeheartedly
joined a muscular, yet quite fun-loving people.

Still a teenager, he rented a cottage,
goateed his beard and allowed his hair
be long and luxurious. The dancier maidens
of his new village, irresisted.

The harbour's fishermen hired him,
and liked him, and he liked them,
learning quickly how vast water endears,
liberating an immediate sense of accomplishment.

Losing timidity in rough seas
cured his dread of men gone mean;
and making a life by wind and clouds,
his confidence grew, his course endured.

He thought he'd become a poet
and fish his way around the globe...
but he never left Lake Erie, and to this day,
fisher-folk call him *"The poet"*, poets call him
"The fisherman".

II

When fisherman was still a lad,
was a prayerful, yet vulnerable youth,
an impatient spirit detoured by place,
wizening over and over and over,
the way waves polish pebbles in the surf
and test the welds of working boats.

There were issues, of course, and many,
he just won't bother recalling nonsense parts,
ignoring nasty repetitions of malicious gossip.
Fisherman has somehow managed to survive
some heroic mandate from above, mellowing
comfortably in his habitat beside the beach.

What mattered to fisherman matters to the soul:
soul work, soul play, soul food, soul mates, old souls
and soul mending, manifesting throughout each season
year after year after year until
everything ignites again come the first of April,
another post-sixtieth marvellous and intimate spring.

Loving his grandchildren loving him,
the poet baubles and coos over babies,
joining kids bubble-blowing among garden flowers.
Somewhat tenderized, the old tough,
loves to see his own young families laugh and play,
giggling and teasing, dancing to silly songs with Papa.

The Spring Street Gang

(my cottage in Erie Rest - 1977, '78)

We were alley-cats
and inquisitive angels
within the same bodies

at our safe-place happily consuming new freedoms

those playful intimacies
where I learned to love her
and her and she as well

loving was all we had and was tremendous fun

among our family of pals
us cool guys and gals
O how we loved one another!

how we thought such love would be ours forever

that couple years so rich with friends
itself seeming like a decade in time
as we emerged from being teens

knowing that no-matter-what we'd always be groovy

laughing together
getting high together —
still held together by old now classic rock songs

Friday Night at the Clifton Hotel

(Port Stanley, the 1980's)

A young fisherman is dancing
in shore boots and jeans still smelling
a bit spontaneously fish-boaty

having not made it home from the lake
he dined instead on fries and suds
his mop of long hair unshowered

and he's not alone in this
with other fishermen happily staying
in the pub as the band starts playing

among farming sons and soddy sorts
the pool-table busy the barmaids busy
as fish plant ladies eye and get eyed

tantalizing on the dance-floor cheering
after each song and hurraying what's next
loosening knots that tether inhibitions

and that young fisherman keeps dancing
like King David in the presence of glory
no longer a body but a dancing soul

dancing with anyone dancing with everyone
his face performing exaggerations of play
with pirouettes and leaps and a few comic collisions

as captains and deckhands stomp in boozy rhythms
while farmworkers prefer their grooving kinda shy
and dancers bounce and sweat laughing as they get untied

Going to Work

(Stanley Harbour, before
the downsizing of a new century)

The crews walk, or ride, or drive,
toward the summons of giant diesels firing—
those first belchings of white smoke
as engines yawn, then cycle, then warm,
blending and settling in a haze of exhausts,
a few hours before night ends.

A dozen local tugs join another dozen or so
from Dover and Maitland, Wheatley and Erieaux—
the fleet increasing as the fishing improves,
fanning-out from port, twinkling like a village on
intercept courses, radios chatting among gentlemen;
nav-lights glowing; compasses, radars, sonars aglow
in the darkness, where values measured by tons
swim beneath the moon, beneath broad hulls shoving
lively water, leaving wakes that sparkle as they churn.

This daily event, ancient as families,
old as millenia, differing from ancestors
only in the noises we make, the hunt is the same:
the quest balancing sufficiency with labour efficiency;
yet the work will always be about strength and grip,
as night finishes, grabbing buoys or shooting trawls...
while ashore, lovers awake and babies fuss.

Just Another Day on Lake Erie

Easterly weather brews
a fresh late-summer breeze
causing close and floppy seas
slapping at the harbour's buoys
as fish-tug lights bounce outbound
into the dark and hollow expanse

of a sullen starless pre-morning
mocking the autopilot lock-on
as it over-corrects ploddingly
plotting stern-quarter rolling wallows
heading west by sou' west toward
pickerel browsing a couple hours out

The grey dawn brings a following
of moping gulls hoping for junk
while the puller-winch toils and rattles
and the lines-coiling crew tattles
on a missing deckhand who had professed
a pub-prophesy of *"wasting time in the slime"*

but the nets are wind-whipping clean
and the fish are twine-kicking green
not heavy though a smiling steady
and with our *'jonah's yap'* workmate ashore
the men are playful and teasing
becoming rather pleasant with the change

The wind reshuffles the long-ponded lake
as a cooler sun silvers in the boat's wake
ending hot weeks of fly-biting doldrums
proving east is not least among winds
that simple persistence does payoff
with luck and skill and a little faith

and so the day goes showing promise
almost filling a few ice-packed totes
as miles of jugged-up nets get set back
about the same fathom-strings as the pull
trading a bit of pain for a lot of pride
while the bow punches that couple hours home

When

"Why are fish-tugs built like tanks?"
—common question

When women walk backwards
wearing dresses gripped by wind gusts
and townsmen hold tight to the brim
of a favourite sport's cap

When a dusty grit rounds corners
causing squinting to see ahead
and harbour water rises and falls
in big swallows beneath the bridge

When green leaves show silver sides
the roots of trees digging deeper
and grounded squirrels go shuffling
anticipating boons in their wealth

When waterfowl head inland
gathering in fields of huddled flocks
and beachgoers remain in their cars
while mounting waves close the pier

When villagers greet behind shop doors
ducking showers blown into splinters
and the summer flags begin to tatter
and sand dunes across the beach-turnabout

When docks get stocked with totes
the trucks with extra ice off-loading
and fish-tug crews return *"Hoo Hoo!"*
with facts better than pub fictions

That's when the money fishing
really gets going out there where
the waves come volley by volley
building toward November's valley by valley

Waiting for the Engine to Cool

I'm aboard the gill-netter *'Iron Fish'*
afterhours
waiting for the engine to cool
to go below and change its oil and filters

but first I'm sipping a beer or two
chain-smoking and talking to myself
like the watchful pleasure of a solitary pike

Here's when a man can bask in satisfaction
with a pack of nicotines
a reliable brass lighter
a razor sharp jack-knife
and a comfortable denim work jacket
like a uniform of the proletariat
that matches well any cap I'm wearing
enjoying my command in a close community

The vessel is well tethered
with a controlled freedom bucking
upon the harbour swells
this private time
with the company's tug
this grey afternoon in late November
musing and looking ahead
to another long winter

I am the next generation
of future oldtimers
my belly thickening with accomplishment
along with tales and prophecies
and understated humour
the best stories becoming legendary
and this season as all others before tells
as many as will fill winter while mending nets

Nothing in earlier life
prepared me for ever-changing routines
endeavouring where-it-takes-ya
whether treacherous ice-coating seas
or a hot day swarming with biting horn flies
for it's fish rather than any conditions that matter
and there's always more than one target to fish for
so many fish in fact
I wonder what keeps 'em comin'

as I sit on the portside steps
that rise to the wheel
smoking and sipping
watching sightseers
drive past me and my boat
a jockey and his antsy thoroughbred

I get up and adjust the dock ties
loosening a couple
snugging up on a couple more
in anticipation of the storm surge
expected tonight

all our nets and gear on dock and deck
nothing left in the lake
tomorrow and the next day off for the crew

Let 'er blow!!
Let 'er stir the mud
the mussels the reeking bones
into a wild sweep clearing the lake bottom
We're playing it safe this time
from the forecasted two-dayer...
an extra day to allow for extra play
followed by if smart
a full day to heal

These nets
there must be twenty years straining the sidelines
twenty years of flapping seagulls' wings
who knows how many thousand gloves worn through
And there's no count of the twine's refillings
of these for now mostly perch nets
only the tallies of fluctuating prices
regardless of the gales and dumped junk fish
and the number of hands who've come and gone

I began my career responsible for these weary nets
and I no longer fear yet do respect the wind
no longer embellish my fishing worthiness
as younger fishermen are apt
I just am what I am
and do what I must do
centered in an old *'Constellation'* compass

balancing on the whirling-bouncing pivot
head-to to quarter-to quarter-before stern-with
bitchin-in-th'-ditch while distributing deck weight
at all times living moment by moment
as a captain both wheeling and working on deck
always from necessity keenly listening
for another's lucky halleluyah on the marine-radio
or a wink and "you-betchya" in the pub among skippers

I chug down the last of my beer
as the engine has cooled enough
Now's time to make the ratchet click

as I'm still thinking amazing how
we bust our asses
week after week after week
chasing after those booster days in-between
when heaping trays of nets are flopping with fish
and we shout *Hurray!* for the glorious pay

Dear CIBC
the cheque is forthcoming
our kids will have new mitts new boots
and presents under the Christmas tree

And me and my beautiful Della
will hire a babysitting neighbour girl
for a night out bumping into friendly faces
dining and *hoppin-around-town*
dancing like foreplay

More to the Story
(for Mark)

I

My brother revells in retelling
a fun sibling-rivalry story
from our early twenties
which I am now appending
forty years later
and the story goes something like this:

He's a polished soldier
with Calgary's *'Lord Strathcona Horse'*
on leave visiting Ontario family
and dropping by to see me
his Port Stanley fisherman brother
all pumped-up by his visit
and itching for a proper good time

So off we go
to my favourite pub
on the eve of a harbour holiday
where the bar-taps are pouring
like an adrenaline-rush
with dancers rockin and braggers talkin
and the only well-heard words are shouts
as I introduce my clean-cut brother
to boisterous long-haired gill-netters who
he compares to the *'Star Trek'* Klingons
arm-wrestling and shooting pool
with popeye-muscled arms
bulging with veins and tattoos

while the ladies wiggle
and mingle and roll their eyes
over silly guys

We partied hearty
table-hopping and barstool bantering
ordering a couple more beers each
fulfilling last-call
my good friend and owner of the place
finally locking-up behind us
not quite not yet falling-over drunk
tripping and laughing in moonlight
along the quiet road home

He passes out on the couch
and me on the rug
him dreaming about army tanks
and me about fishing tugs —
now here's where the story gets good
as it should and did and has:

He leaps up in the a.m. early
with the birds (and who-knows
maybe frolicking butterflies)
going for an apparently daily
ten-klick military run followed by
a return ten-klick sightseeing jog
(even racing a dog)
arriving well refreshed
to a big bacon and eggs breakfast
with his new sister-in-law

As for me
I'm a thump of dropped lead
anchored to the floor
thankful for the wee mercy
of a pillow under my head
which helps contain a nauseating whirling
as I seriously object to
even a suggestion of opening curtains

And wow does my brother loom large
like some kinda halleluyah miracle
(or a freak of nature)
proudly popping an after-coffee beer
shattering the infamous long-held myth
and proving a fact
that a soldier's physical fitness triumphs
over any hippie fisherman's fabled capacity
at least in this instance
when the Wilson clan's two oldest boys
put our viking-irish on
trading widowmaker threatening tales
of close-call combats and stormy seas
going to-to-toe having a blast
with me at the end sorely
tapping out

II

After four decades
of silent sibling diplomacy:

I'd worked the day my brother showed
waking hours before sunrise
and that notorious next morning
was my first day off in more than twenty
hauling nets and laying nets and picking
entangled fish quick-as-we-can
muscling with concentrated skill
one fish at a time ton after ton after ton
bouncing around on Lake Erie
sorting through miles and miles of coiling rope
and twine and anchors and floats and buoys
all stitched together with high-speed knots
while busting and shovelling and packing boatloads
then truckloads of ice keeping our product chilled...

I'd also been stepping outside
(sans brother)
throughout that night sharing puffs
in a huddle of pals
kissing down big fatty reefers
celebrating our deckhand moxie
while easing somewhat the burning pain
of swollen fish-poisoned fingers
with generous swigs from a *jug 'a shine*
and special *skinnies* twisted with
some hurry-back-in kickass bud—

jus' sayin

The Work of Art

(in memory of
Captain Arthur Grayling)

About what so-and-so said
he'd say *"I've forgotten more*
about how to fish Lake Erie
than that jerk probably knows"

and this wasn't bragging but a fact
as I worked formative years with him
heeding stuff like *"next time bruise your boots*
you need those fightin-fists for fishin'"

and among storm-force towering seas
I asked *"we gonna make it home?"*
he said *"just put a brand new keg on ice*
I'll be damned if I'm leavin it to my wife!"

Mastering the art of *"dragging lures"*
he retired his tug and fresh-fish business
designing an ideal charter-fishing boat
to harvest the smiles of adventurous folk

while carrying the weight
of a man a full foot taller
and sporting the beaming grin
of a fella much wider

endearing his wife and then
*un*dearing his wife and again
endearing his wife all within
a single hour as I recall

and he was that way with anyone
even an angered opponent who
at some aside moment did
find mercy over a cold brew

as he was one with his word
a comical word mindya rarely
saying *love* but kindness was
the method by which he breathed

showing a much younger me
by example how real courage
allows for laughter in a mighty gale
how humour itself can always heal

In a world taunted by egos
in a town tortured by gossip
not many faces shone like his
sharing light with lifelong pals

as his heart enlarged
to such a spanse no matter
how tough his hands his body
could no longer contain it

and oh how I miss him
my mentor and a best friend
thirty years my senior—
nary a day goes by

Jackie Grayling

(for Heather)

My dead buddy's wife,
a fisherman's widow, is elderly
and ill and stubborn as an old scar.
With curly white hair nicely done,
her one good eye clear and bright,
 greets me with a hug and kiss.

I've brought a six-pack of *'Blue Light'*
to reminisce, in our shared vernacular, stories
so captivating there's no need for embellishment,
as fine antlers and mounted fish adorn the walls,
inspiring tales and approve the telling.
Photos of *"the skipper"* in typically jolly spirit,

seem as if he's about to walk right in
with a *"guess who's here!"* guest for supper.
He was a legendary Lake Erie captain,
a generous, unconditionally hospitable fella—
she never begrudged him that;
nor later, in semi-retirement, side by side,

before sunrise, until lunch, mending nets:
'semblin needles 'digging, inch by inch,
"walkin backwards" along the twine-stretch, finishing up
with a radio country song wee twirl of a dance.
He had his boats, for her, the fresh-fillet shop;
a smart daughter and a couple tall grandsons

completed them. Dear memories
associate each souvenir and trophy in its place,
proudly displayed and suspended in time;
and a fat black lab named Spot, who,
in people years, might be pushing a hundred,
nudges my hand and wags her tail.

Jackie is, apparently, reluctant to budge,
for fear, I think, of having to adjust
to residence among *"those weird city-folks"*;
of leaving the breath and music of the lake;
of having to shed what's untranslatable—
that, she does her husband grudge.

Robert 'Silly' Tilly

He was pleasant drunk
and just as pleasant sober—
I liked him

got to workin with him fishin
Lake Erie outa Port Stanley aboard
'Marvelous' Marvin Berry's gill-netter *'Mi Mar Lynn'*

where Tilly took me under his wing
honing skills I'd been practising on other tugs
refining better how-tos and the best what-knots

where sluggin on the lake trumps life ashore
yet there's more to life than just fishin
there's beer there's women and enjoying the view

as I was a ways yet from his experience with
a scolding ex-wife or stern men who don't like beer
a ways yet from the mastery moving his arms

"'cause if you can fish you'll never go hungry"
and although we seem governed by frauds and fools
a good-ole silly soul can speak truer than most

and don't bother embellishing too much a good story
since the fishin itself makes tales tall enough
that cherished stories are what chapter us

that people talk the way they talk
"'cause they might have a bad case of the blues"
then any beer brand is a good beer handed chilled

and I'm remembering his joviality
his quick and keenly observant sense of humour
how he could heed a strong woman elbowing his ribs

"'cause a good gal is tricky to find"
and trickier to stay with—
she's got moods

like the lake's got moods
the reason it's called a *'she'*
eventually getting fishermen right like it or not

Over many seasons through storm and shine
we worked and laughed together off and on
a same boat or from another along the ports

as we kept in touch with
death of a friend or a grandchild's arrival...
and he never forgot my birthday

Fisherman's Beach

I know a place
in fair weather west of Port Stanley
past the cliffs and rounding Plum Point
that inspires a rather uncommon
sort of appreciation in being here
aboard a local Lake Erie gill-net tug
many years worthy of its proud name
and from a working deck's perspective
gazing shoreward out busy doors
at the sprawling ever-changing scenery
where one might catch a wistful glimpse
of an old fisherman's spirit lingering
just before he enters heaven

and it's pleasantly cool
with autumn hinting in the breeze
across the inner bight of a wide bay
as the morning haul rewards with perch
while land lounges above sloping banks
with cornfields and nut-bearing forests
and the sun is clearly delighted
charmfully glittering calm water
exposing a hidden beach secluded where
a young fisherman might return
to set a tent below the Milky Way
and his body overwhelm the soul
with a lover

Tough-guys

Two middle-aged net fishermen,
just off the lake, supposedly relaxing,
are instead, persisting in a confrontation
that threatens physical combat...
beer gut to burly beer gut,
whiskery faces, in each other's face,
got their prides caught in too many beers,
imagining themselves fist-fighters;
and perhaps they are, or once were.

Pairs of balls, a pair of bulls,
stare down the other's tunnel vision,
tempting trouble with *"Yer nothin but fuckin yap!"*
responded by *"Okay then, let's fuckin dance!"*
as they go on, flirting with eruption...
sons of the lake, sons of the pub,
are still shoving in a schoolyard,
engaging in the sport of insulting words,
puffing chests and rolling-back sleeves,
as their women, with *no-more-nonsense*, intervene.

Equals in spirit, equals in mastery,
each defending his own fundamental narrative,
within which, colossally weathered character
emboldened by habit with ornery encounters,
compete, and sometimes, apparently, conflict...
will seek peace when sober and sore,
like sorry brothers snared by some quarrel
that no longer makes as much sense as it seemed
when testosterone triggered an adrenaline pop.

A Near-Death Experience

Remember when fishin
was so good
we could afford t'drink
't'killya' outa water glasses?

One night I got stuck
in th' phone booth...
you know
th' one was outside
the ole red dog.
Had t'call a buddy
come get me out!

That was th'year 'a my
second divorce
when I lost my fishin job
findin work as a fill-in...
just fell in a crack
and kinda lost track.

Did about a two-year thing
gettin gibbled everyday
on cheap wine 'n other stuff...
it wound-up killin
my best friend then.
Fuckin' near killed me!

Got sick for a couple 'a months
my skin turnin yella...
couldn't even see
th'whites 'a my eyes!

All She Really Needed

The neighborhood bar
is annoyingly noisy and
getting louder by the minute
as I'm listening less
to the words and more
to her eyes...

to his sins that sank them
into the well of her skull
her reddening eyes
speaking volumes along with
how she got fucked up and
if it wasn't for her grandmother...

and I'm feeling protective

of her lovely eyes
her desperate proximity her
sullen tyranny in
my personal space...
so I touch her
pulling gently at her elbow

inviting her to dance
allowing an anonymous moment
for a few sheltering minutes
to slowly dance with her now smiling eyes...
which is after all that telling
all she really needed

A Love Story

(Grimmond's Beach, Port Stanley)

We live beside a Great Lake
yet our loving is big as the biggest sea
and that sea adores bird-soaring skies
where such a view renews with always light

And the light is shining on children
seeming to glow with popcorn in their hands
with mommy and daddy and gramma and grampa
on their little bright smiling lips

And we play with beach between our toes
building castles with moats and stones and feathers
digging shovelsfull into pails and getting sand in our hair
from cooling bouncing swims among sparkling waves

And the sky awaits with its always here
where loved ones arrive with those they love most
sunbathing and picnicking and kiting in a breeze
as we share seasons with crowds loving likewise

And there are endless wonders to discover
this close to the lake we call home
close to that sea where our anchors hold
listening to deep water while gazing at clouds

And we laugh and dance and feast and thrive
'cause that's the way it's always been
living and loving our lives
this side of town

Lake Erie, My Lake

for Harrison

It's been about ten?
long detoured years
                                since
I fished

hauling nets all over the lake
working upon my lake
and it is
            my lake

according to
my little grandson pointing
and making a point:

"Papa's Lake!"

I see what he's saying

hear the gulls and lapping waves
the sunlight blinking upon water...
and there are so many *upons*
decades of upons
from the wheelhouse of my memory.

He heard those bold words from cousins

and now he sees it
shining like some huge answer
beside me
holding my hand.

Stagecraft

Rathering

In the search for
or rather a hoping for freshening
some aspect of the spirit of truth

or that conundrum with multiple truths
or maybe some increased access to
energies and odd remedies or fantastic visions

as if through signs and portents or what-have-you...
that curious passion for longings and hungers
or rather more obscurable mysteries and wonders

wandering and pondering and weighing
mulling over thoughts almost worth sharing
or perhaps just out-and-about paddling a canoe

contemplating life and transcendence
in other words verifying the latest news
of acidity versus passivity... with empathy

in other words navigating things in common
or rather wealth commonly available
that is as opposed to what's conjured

as when springtime assembles thens with nows
more comprehending rather than revising matters
that've been agitating and swelling for months

or rather never failing to surprise
rendering as if unquestionably benign...
let's call it the month of May

and to reduce rathering to a singular event
(a drum-roll if you please) that
noble yet ordinary sign among indications—

'Gone Fishin'

The Southern Dunwich
Jefferson Salamander

(Letter to Pud Hunter,
biologist, OMNR)

Unlike the loss of a longtime friend,
a sacred place has passed
without a lingering spirit to keep dear
and be watched over by.
A place of low rank,
it starkly disappeared.
I am grieving

over my wildflower scented,
most treasured woods;
and a distinctly jewelled
population of Jefferson Salamanders,
endemic to timbered swamps, were surviving
where the Talbot Creek watershed
elbows Lake Erie.

An unconscionably rare,
couple dozen acres, was ripped apart
just this past winter.
The new lease-farmer said
to a pal of mine,

> *"Gotta get this swamp*
> *outa here*
> *before somebody tries to stop me!"*

O how my children loved to uncover,
and feed worms to, those pleasant sports
with their starlight-blue spangles.
Shining skin, cool as early morning plums,
they had the soft bellies of an easy life;
their eyes, purely pupils, poking atop
big cartoon-like smiles; their feet, like hands
of teeny-weeny people, climbing our fingers.

A log must mellow for years to house one,
a perennial resident, which could be returned to
and fed again, and given a name
like *Godzilla*, or *Sammy*, or *Mr. Wrinkles*;
and not just them, also
the hefty, broader ranging Yellow-spotted,
and some elfin, hillside dwelling salamanders:
the Red-back and the Four-toed.

An accident of geography
preserved them an extra hundred and fifty years,
beyond the footfalls of mastodons and giant beavers,
then deer and horses and cattle; a pocket wetland
bordered by cash-crops below timbered ridges.

I wrote some of my favourite poems there
upon its logs, beneath budding skies,
frog listening.

Corn leaves wave farewell in the wind.
False green whispers like fake syllables.
Rain falls and the mud is just mud.
It has become a plain of puddles and pests.

I wish I had, at least once,
spent a whole night resolving,
by flashlight,
the moon's intimate mirages
from tiny glistening eyes
among the wood-lichens, quietly walking
around those breeding pools
in a mild April wet spell.
I wish you, or myself,
had owned the deed to that land.

Dear Pud,
I am much saddened to report:
a wide assortment of species, holding out
in that final vestige, (such a small corner

of suitable habitat) are currently extirpated
from the district; or moved on as refugees
competing over other's territory. And as for
the Dunwich variant of *'Ambystoma Jeffersonianum'*,
(what an unnecessary erasure!)
now, quite possibly, extinct.

Two Trees and a Spider

The spring breeze moves more freely here
where two tall trees have widely conspired
allowing only a lushness of low growth
by capturing the overhead forest together—
sisters I suppose and a type of oak likely
with acorn debris strewn across the duff
though a few days too early in the season
to identify budding leaves not yet unfolded

When suddenly through the branches
a slant of mid-morning light ignites
the longest and thickest spider thread
I have anywhere ever bumped into
from one trunk to the other at face height
like a zip line and nearly as tough
as I pluck at it and then pluck again
seeming to relay some informative note

What arachnid could hang such a wire
and for such a curious webless purpose?
Was it pulled or someway blown between
spanning about a dozen long-step paces ?
How powerful a body? How awful those jaws?
And why did loggers ignore these fine timbers
doubling one another as if in a gigantic mirror?
Whose blessing or conjuring preserves them?

Somehow hidden in someone's back forty
Is a bower that might invite lovers to kiss
In an old unlogged knoll of a place
where maybe a monster spider persists
stapling a claim between broadly rooted columns
lying in ambush from some shadow hereabout
to pounce upon and proceed with shrivelling
a mouse or a bird... or a stray cat perhaps

Woodlots

I

Here, and there, the tidy woodlots
of southwestern Ontario continue to provide
lean refuge for cloistered, lean adapted species
hiding amid the barest allowances, squarely
settled, within roaded grids boxed in survey-minutes,
kept honest minutes, European minutes, overlorded
by accomplices of divinity, by manifest destiny
shuffling territories from the preconquistadorian,
continental soul where

survivors reserve some rights to shadows:
snakes, for example, risking their summer lives
trespassing for a bask in sunlight; or *The People*,
the treaty-peoples' reminding, so so-drummingly,
about preserving their say, though only woodlots
remain around small swamps, along muddied creeks;
a Carolinian character of rare, heirloom trees
and brilliantly warbling, diminishing birds
trying their damndest

to nest, despite whittlings and diversions,
as modern farming too, with virtuous abundance,
bows before *Urbania*; the hemispherics of climate
growing dustier way beyond widely vastering cities;
our woodlots becoming increasingly interplanetary.
How recover, maybe even reconnect, scarred remnants
of biodiversity hoping to maintain viable dimensions?
Woods are still hallowed; it's not yet too late!
Good people know this.

II

Within the woods, one might rediscover relic haunts
and childhood textures, of change among sameness,
as if instantly renewed and just as ever wondrous;
again exploring, quite distractedly, along that path
where only rubber boots and pockets were necessary.

Developing contemplative tendencies, one may view,
and accompany vision, with an attendant gratitude
enhanced by stillness, as keener listening magnifies
seeing with much farther and detailed and surprising
awareness: that wanderings tramp upon sacred ground.

Eventually, one acquires binoculars and comfortable
hiking shoes; a small pack including illustrations
guidebooking, page-turningly, an excited child's
chatty inquisitiveness; how trees invite a deeper
delving into littler lives dwelling under old logs.

And, of course, one witnesses flightier moments:
the way deer startle, huffingly, with bright, white
tails bouncing away; or a big, red-headed fox snake
sunning, trancelike, its fat length upon the trail,
reluctantly sliding beneath a foliage full of wings.

One returns to one's usual world somewhat echoed
by loftiness and charmed breathing, by a sense of
something released and something of spirit kept:
where bug pestered shade strengthens perseverance;
that green and mottled light *most* venerates the sun.

A Sheaf of Sonnets:

Drama At The Beach

Finding myself at this moment
somewhat startled by a kind of
giddy panic realizing I've
currently gone doddery somehow
when I quite amusingly just now
seem to have preferred gazing upon

a view more pleasing a dying man
rallied by sunlight so beamingly
through dark clouds glowing cathedrally
sparkling the lake midst columns of shade

rather than those two lovely ladies
almost ignored while jogging right there
so shapefully hipped and bummingly
with long strong legs and flowing hair

Mimicking

What fun is a toddler pointing at
when one or two words have to make do
while inviting you to do pointing too
for what dearer a noun is such as that
now closely mimicked by a littler you
whether a blossom or a bird or a star
a fruit or a toy or an outstanding colour
the details aren't entirely in just looking

when suddenly here's a grasped and handed thing
a fleeting texture that might have a quick taste
for must as a child *sees* then grabs in haste
asking what or why or who from primary you
the game often simply concludes with a *Wow*
since not going on about when or where or how

First Tomato

for mom

The earliest harbingers of autumns
clamouring within their ripening dream
like grapes and berries and sunnyside plums
but emblazoned by a much bolder theme
with galaxies of fields or just one plant
reddened with stars and whirling stars at that
spinning on the twirling of the planet
growing round and round and getting quite fat
this first ripe tomato plucked from the stem
smelling that freshly parted scent release
so plump to the touch still warm from the sun
now cutting slice upon thinly sliced piece
    remembering us with each summer's first
    on the knife-edge of the best taste on toast

Crow Country

(in memory of my mentor)

I'm happiest in the regions of crows
in autumn when the fat deer are feisty
tasting air in the hills of farm country
following game trails just above the rows

now here we are again my spirit friend
trimming shooting-lanes for opening-morn
between blowdowns and weeds near standing corn
reading woods while according with the wind

while stepping along with talkative crows
nitpicking over this and over that
remarking quite boldly amongst themselves
perhaps about me wearing your old hat
   in this evening of echoes and these crows
   recalling us accompanied by those

Afterglow

"... and in the resurrection of the dead
will neither marry nor be given in marriage."
(Luke: 20:35 NCV)

Memory, sweet memory, remember
  those generous bodies who pleasured me
as I groomed my first beards; remain tender,
  O private garden of love's history!

Recall the scent of warm, feminine skin,
  on top of one, or beneath another,
for I was a pheromone junkie then,
  dipped in afterglow, chatting together.

I've never quite erased love's forgotten
  faces from my youth's premarital stint;
since long decades have grown post-begotten,
  I now allow my thoughts this wayward hint:
a quiet permission to bless the past,
  when all glows again, like angels, at last.

Lust, As Love With Need

Lust, as love with need, gladdens in a test,
touchably freed, while sharing between a pair
kindly daring... is better finding such rest:
when flesh, overjoyed by moisturized verbs,
wanes toweled and content with tenderized words.
Lust, as love, is splendid, best expressed where
earned caresses finesse those playful requests
well intended; now they're dancing, much blessed.

Yet lust, with boredom, can get upended,
turning otherwise depends, if attended,
upon a slyer touch which may not be blessed;
then lust, unlike love, risks getting unwieldy,
now mistaking, or forsaking love, wanes needy,
ever more seedy, like a ghost, becomes a pest.

Woodstock Festival, 1969

(on the fiftieth anniversary)

The crowding grew famous, or infamous,
  "either way's groovy", said hippies to not;
  loud, athletic music, often zealous,
  sought adversity to malicious thought.
Although mid-summer, both sunny and wet,
  their spirits applauded eternal spring,
  spreading welcome beyond the continent
  with a kind, and contagious, peaceful thing.

Almost half a million young, was the talk,
  perceiving themselves as old souls at play,
  dancing in the mud outside of Woodstock,
  sharing fellowship by moon and by day.
Despite an unfettered sporting with dope,
  they fancied a future then filled with hope.

New Moon

So calm,
just one tree
frog calls,
beneath neon
planets, the hoodied
new moon, and yonder
lies the city's blooming
bubble of glow

Stars show
brighter flames
this night, more
sentient, more
seductively each
with each other,
with whatever names
I can remember

Ursa Minor,
seldom shining, shines
now, momentously
with kin for its
immobile star, now
little dipper, now
found easily by way
of its mother

Come out to
our yard, my love,
my lovest, and gaze
at this twinkling,
vaster display of
cool, gentler lights,
so romantically
winking

See how
faint, yet how
teamingly clear,
the galaxy's glowing,
everflowing arm, tips
its dizzy avenue
across and over to
Sagittarius

Only a tracing of
moon, a rim's trace,
yet fullness abides
in dimness, inside
itself, its face
erased, at rest,
like an empty
nest

Post-Glacial

(in memory of
Carl Sagan and Stephen Hawking)

All of cosmology sprawls before me
on this lake's beach its wavy parallels aligned
lengthwise by driftwoods and sorted by weight
with evidences reckoning vast timeframes
I can barely imagine yet plainly see

these gravels the grinding stars of this place
once oceans that later arose as mountains
eroding into slaughtered hills over widening plains
leaving photos on polished stones the becomings
life long toyed-with in a baby-step space

Even light gets bent at water's edge
blending rocks and rubbish with the worn-out
which flip until boned and particle the roots
of grasses first then up poppling trees
as only inclemencies fulfill such a pledge

while millions upon billions glitter underfoot
smaller and smaller until again bittings build
finding me strolling along the sandier parts
feeling smart and hot and cooling my feet
I pick up a little wonder enduring where put

Attending an Outdoor Book Launch

We're not yet finished hearing the first poem
and I'm just catching a mere gist of its winding up
as a three-star gold-sticker although rather ambling piece
    because limitingly for me
this is an outdoor garden-of-delights venue
with robins and cardinals singing like gang-rappers
and I'm mostly deaf in my right ear anyway
as this stool of a chair seats me in the left groin
    of the garden
My oh my I must have some kinda crush on poetry
enduring an ache booting me in the spine while witnessing
this effectfully read and quite entertaining performance
because despite the many occurring distractions
there are lots of smiling approvals and I'm discerning the poet's
    well-versed in natural light
making legit this mental-yoga thing going on
these gentle folk appearing more cerebrally fit at focusing ears
than my apparent lack at comprehensive multi-tasking while
    toads are toading trillingly
and dogwood flowers cast scent like a cheap perfume
and the prettiest woman here keeps shooing at her hair
and that constant sniffing behind me seems a bit much
though I am looking forward to buying a signed book and
    as elegance mingles with the tawdry
I'm gonna hang around listening this lovely evening through
while attempting a closer proximity
to things said

If

if a shadow stalls
where none are who
and *if* said shadow stirs
whiffing of tobacco or lavender

if the cat seems jittery
about nothing where nothing is
or the dog in the yard growls
again outside a particular window

if unbodied voices occur
as *if* an incident's echo
if a not-quite someone suddenly
tosses things in bits of fits

if a room vacates over a child's fears
heavy with its own peculiar weight
or a garden rain falls too oddly moody
as *if* too much like sullen tears

if the sun shrinks and goes strangely wan
or the moon hoods its normal muse
if silence startles with uncaused hurt
and feelings go from weird to weirder

if rogue movements duck
if house-plants refuse to flourish
if a cold chill pauses with a poke
or a lock of hair gets plucked

if something less
chooses something more
knocking on a wall or a door
whether *if* ignored or not

and *if* what from out
slips its way in
persisting as *if* insisting upon
leaving that door ajar

then *if* glimpsed or *if* spotted
point quickly shouting *There!*
that empty stare in mid-air always
plays this game as always
too late

Sapiens Sapiens

Slowly but surely evolving we
gaze upon some clever thing
(cave art or a picasso or e.e. cummings)
and are helplessly amazed
delighting in quirky genius

unlike those other sapiens our
neanderthalensis brethren who
(fur clad in deep snow yet bare-footed?)
were way too practical while we
went tinkering among visions

beyond the game-scented breeze
seeing a sea as if beckoning
(with cherubs and dragons sporting wings)
looking at *who-knows-where*
and actually getting there

Favouring the madly courageous
contagiously crazy genes we
(dancing like peacocks in transcendence)
sought after curiosities which
were rare and new and best

and now we are everywhere
improving upon our shiniest
(high-definition-wireless controlled)
most frightening achievement—
the mirror on the wall

Angels Fallenly

"You are *why* you are
stuck as you are—
a mighty sticky matter!"
says cousin Uriel with
flaming sword barring
the hairy lot of us
who've chosen
(quite courageously)
both darkly and
glowingly dangerous
hugely short lives
in this vastly universed
house of fallen angels

For us who must eat
from a wobbling earth
making the most out of
sunlight and shadows…
that is this abusively
sweating place of us
having gone must-havingly
(thus the nowing down in time)
consume greedily
therefore predatorially
shall not enter
until abandoning altogether all
matter finally

Original Sin

Over my shoulder
and there it is
the tar featherer
whispering in my ear

as it glories in
making a voice of me
adding to someone's disgrace
by spreading embarrassment

Now I'm superior!

Now appetized for more

backstabbing banter
boosting my clever self
by blistering a reputation
even by dissing the dead

suspending my conscience
among those popular sorts
easily tickled and amused
with ever nastier stuff

Now it's fun!

Now it's inside me

Standing Before His Maker

(his angel's litany)

He never allowed fear to hamper a real concern
never flinched much in a desperate situation
never kept faith with a faith he couldn't die with
never sinned so awfully or so deeply as to sin too far
never was vengeful but for a mean word or two
never punched an asshole who didn't swing first
never drank to the point of an alcoholic need
never failed a personal secret told in confidence
never ignored the needy or avoided the seedy
never argued with authorities without due respect
never fired an employee without giving fair warning
never lied when the truth would serve best
never bragged much but perhaps about a few things
never worried never complained about acquiring stuff
never took up a cause that didn't favour the wounded
never tolerated the presence of a dull knife
never hunted to kill yet did kill to have hunted
never harvested anything without reverential care
never had sex with a gal who didn't want to
never shacked up with a woman he couldn't marry
never wore jewellery that wasn't a beloved's gift
never claimed to be a better lover or a better friend
never loved perfectly yet loved from his best
never took family for granted never loved anyone less
and he didn't cave or despair over the illness
that broke him

Poem Split in Two

I

I've been enlightened
many times
and yet enlightenment
eludes me

Once was a time
and then again
then at another place
seemed a bit nearer

then wasn't
what I expected when
darkness overwhelmed
and I sought shelter from

what's inwardly inkled
but by overthinking
denies any furtherance
leaving me perplexed

and so I am not
inspired over this poem
although I pursue this
nonetheless

Silly eh?
making a blank page
blanker by the line
this pit of a poem

if even that much and yet you're reading this
as I'm writing this
somewhat sensing something tricky

and now we're curious
how this might finish...
maybe a peg some way
that we can *"hang a hat on"*

So here it is
best I can come up with
without any furtherance—

my spirit aches for us

II

Only a moment later
a phone call...
Baird 'The Bearcat' Reeves
my best man
and lifelong fishing buddy

has suddenly died

I wept for hours

and still am...

A coincidental spinning? just prior to
was already in that stream of consciousness
(doing what I *usually* enjoy doing)
when pencil and pad and an odd premonition?
went from puzzled
               to brittle
                    to a wrenched empty
(followed by a punched
despairingly dented innocent
wall)

From earliest teens to entering our sixties
so many adventures and a few misadventures
the loudest laughter and a few quiet tears
always (even early this troubled morning)
shared with each other...

to here now
quite unexpectedly
sitting helpless in the dark
after that initial ache
                    vaultingly
manifested
into the immediate awfulness
of grief...
and I suspect this agony
will never go away

over the *gone* of my boisterous Baird

Autobiography of My Legs

(But Jacob said, "I will not let you go
unless you bless me." - Genesis, 32)

My legs were uneven
resulting from a childhood hockey injury
that split my hip
for I was a scruffy little guy playing among
scrappy little guys
on unregulated and spontaneously unparented surfaces

My legs continued uneven
walking with a confident but somewhat clipped manner
like a signature
like a chip-shouldering swagger from meaner streets
(or so they said)
when I carried a positive yet dangerous way about me

My legs pursued leg challenges
finding their niche in a hard-working career choice
earning seaworthiness
for captaining fishing vessels muscling on Lake Erie
contending with rugged men
handling and losing and repairing tough priorities

My legs enjoyed less gravity
when rolling around wrapped within legs of lovers
until one lover
proved beyond doubt to be lovest of all loves
healing my missteps
with a firm fidelity erasing unholy parts of my past

Our legs sprouted legs
little legs at first then growing to full maturity
of sons and daughters
baptized and raised and confirmed as children of God
whose grace somehow always
overcame rudenesses and growling words from ill spirits

My legs are now more uneven
having accumulated a lifetime of annoying injuries
including one too many
fielding me with an intolerably unbalanced swayback
and despite my cane
our beautiful grandkids still think I can walk on water

A Final Word

Some words cling like burrs in a meadow,
like popcorn fragments stuck in teeth; or like honey,
sticky with a licky taste lingering on fingers—
because the gluiest words find fervour and renewal
scrutinized by devotees reading and hymning together,
binding volumes with centuries and favouring leather:

and it's also common taking words for granted,
as when preferring gaming over intimate dialogue,
thinking *"Oh god, what have I gone and neglected?"*
and yet, proceed to disregard whimsy and depth and height,
because capacity is limited and limited words shed tiny light;
let poets do the fanciful; let bards fly with birds:

and there will always be betrayers and betrayed,
the leavers and the stayed, scarringly polarizing words
because we love to eclipse, despite our common dustiness,
with yays and nays in desperate tribes; or with the angelic,
their eyes pinned to scopes while others preach paradise;
yet, putting words to melody, even foes share delight:

and then those evenings with a bottle of wine,
when embracing looser properties of pensive time,
and for a moment, words don't matter; or too much do,
mulling simmering pejoratives; or just merely listening
to cricking crickets and breezy trees and muttering water...
because witnessing life is looking like a hard act to follow:

Thank You

Author Bio:

Michael J. Wilson has been writing, and identifying himself as a poet, since age thirteen. Reading and writing poetry became his primary focus throughout high school. Immediately after graduating, he began a career in commercial fishing out of Port Stanley on Lake Erie. He liked fishing for a living both for its challenges and rewards, as well as for the winter downtimes since that allowed him free time to concentrate on his writing. His first efforts were published in the village newspaper, "Port Stanley Beacon".

During earlier off-seasons, he took courses at the University of Windsor in order to broaden his knowledge. He also earned a "Fishing Master" certificate, followed by "Master of Minor Water Steamship" from Georgian College, which allowed him to serve as captain, or relief-captain, on types of vessels other than fishing boats. Since those early days his poems appeared periodically in lit-mags, anthologies, and university reviews throughout Canada. His first collection of poems, *Where Rivers Begin* was published by Third Eye Press of London, Ontario in 1996.

In 2006, the documentary film, *Sea Without Tides*, appeared as a broadcast on 'A-Channel' and public television. The film portrayed commercial fishing on Lake Erie as observed through Mike's eyes giving his perspective as both fisherman and poet—he voiced much of the film's narrative using his own poems. In hindsight, Mike sees this film as a *swan song* of his career on the lake. In 2009, three years after the film's release, he was diagnosed with a traumatic, viral brain-injury resulting from a "head bonk" received while working on the lake. A virus invaded his brain and nervous system, leaving him with severe physical and mental deficits.

Mike was forced to retire from his beloved lake, and having to readjust how to read and write, he applied his original work-ethic, on a daily basis, toward "rewiring" his brain: *Still Dancing* is just one example of the results of those efforts. His return to poetry is a miracle and a blessing for which the readers of *Still Dancing* might join in the dance and be joyful.

Mike resides in Port Stanley with his wife, Della. Their four children live in nearby St. Thomas along with seven grandchildren – his favourite accomplishment and the loves of his life.

www.ingramcontent.com/pod-product-compliance
Lightning Source LLC
Chambersburg PA
CBHW031252120626
46545CB00007B/2770